THE BIBLE'S SEVEN PILLARS OF WISDOM

WIPF & STOCK · Eugene, Oregon

David Hamshire

Wipf and Stock Publishers
199 W 8th Ave, Suite 3
Eugene, OR 97401

The Bible's Seven Pillars of Wisdom
By Hamshire, David
Copyright©2017 Apostolos
ISBN 13: 978-1-5326-6924-8
Publication date 9/23/2018
Previously published by Apostolos, 2017

ACKNOWLEDGMENTS

First, I thank Janet, my wife and companion for more than fifty years, for her support during the many hours spent in study and research to bring this booklet into print.

I also thank Margaret Harber, a friend who lives in the village where my wife and I have lived for the last twenty years; and Mike Moore, a long-serving staff member of *'Christian Witness to Israel'*, for their helpful suggestions for the improvement of the original manuscript for this study.

I thank Desi Maxwell, whose ministry I have benefited from, for writing the Foreword. Desi has studied at the University of Ulster and the Westminster and Princeton theological Seminaries. He entered pastoral ministry for seven years – three in Canada, followed by four in Belfast. For twenty years, Desi lectured at Belfast Bible College (and remains a senior teaching fellow) before seeking to bring the classroom to the living room through *'Xplorations'*, the ministry he co-founded and directs with his wife Heather. Given his knowledge and his background, Desi's kind words are more than I could have expected and I am most grateful.

My thanks also include Dr. Ron George, from Crowborough, East Sussex (UK), and Niall MacTaggart, who lives in Spruce Grove, Alberta, Canada. Their friendship since I have known them – although I have not yet had an opportunity to meet Niall face-to-face – has been of a kindred spirit.

Finally, I thank Mathew Bartlett at Apostolos Publishing for his help in publishing this study. This is the third manuscript Matthew has published for me and details of the previous two titles can be found at the end of this book.

THE ALPHA AND OMEGA OF ALL THINGS

In the beginning, God created the heavens and the earth. The earth was without form, and void; and darkness was on the face of the deep. And the Spirit of God was hovering over the face of the waters.

(Genesis 1:1–2)

*In the beginning was the Word,
And the Word was with God,
And the Word was God.
He was in the beginning with God.*

(John 1:1–2)

God, who at various times and in various ways spoke in time past to the fathers by the prophets, has in these last days spoken to us by His Son, whom He has appointed heir of all things, through whom also He made the worlds.

(Hebrews 1:1–2)

FOREWORD

Bible-readers and jam-makers often adopt similar methods. Despite the apparent difference in the two occupations, the inclination is to store the fruits of their labours in neatly sealed units. Readers tend to systematize their findings and file them away in neatly organized mental compartments, while cooks use jam jars to ensure the flavours never mix! Maybe this is a wise decision when it comes to jam making, but it is dreadfully debilitating when it comes to exploring the richness of the Bible.

While we stand indebted to many scholars, much academic study of the Bible is specialized. An *'expert'* on the Hebrew Bible is not allowed to comment on the New Testament, and vice versa. Such is the degree of specialization that the view of the sweeping forest has been obscured by the twigs on the trees. The outcome is to the detriment of us all. Given the fact that Hebrew, the language of the Scriptures, has no word for theology, doctrine or creed, surely alerts us to something? All our attempts to *'organize'* the Bible into rigidly systematic units is rather meaningless. Surely, it's time to take a step back and to look at the text as a whole?

Abraham Heschel once observed that the Greek studies to understand, while the Hebrew studies to revere. Our reverence, and indeed our awe, will certainly only increase as we grow in sensitivity to interconnections of time, place and people in this unique literature. This is what David does in these pages. It's as if he invites us to don a new pair of *'tri-focals'* to see with excitement that no one text can be studied in isolation. No one angle, neither time, place, nor people, will provide a definitive interpretation, but all three combine to give us a high definition insight. The rabbis were often masterful at this and their method sets them apart from our traditional western methods.

As you journey with David, you won't find everything sitting neatly labelled on shelves, ordered with the precision that we've come to expect. That's simply not the way that the Bible was intended to be read.

I invite you to travel with David as he discards the old containers and lets the richness of the flavours mix.

Desi Maxwell
May 2017

INTRODUCTION

The background for this study was carried out prior to my second visit to Chisinau (April 2017), the capital of Moldova. My first visit was in 2016, and the reason I was planning to return was because I had been invited to speak to students at a Christian university.

Dr. Mihai Malancea, President of the *'Universitatea Divitia Gratiae'* (its name translates as, *'The Riches of His Grace'*), had asked me to prepare a series of five lectures for the university's first-year students. The subject for the five lectures was: *'Hebrew Foundations of the Christian Faith'*. My final lecture was to share with the students what is referred to in the Bible as its *'Seven Pillars of Wisdom'*.

The students who attend this university come from a wide-range of countries which were once part of the Soviet Union. The reason they come to Moldova is to obtain a degree level of education in subjects ranging from Christian theology and Semitic languages, to business and social studies.

During my first visit in 2016, I shared with the students then, something of the parallels which can be seen in the *'Seven Days of Creation'* (Genesis 1:1 to 2:3) and the *'Seven Feasts of the Lord'* (Leviticus 23:3–44) – but not the *'Seven Pillars of Wisdom'*.

A few weeks before I was due to return to Moldova, I was asked by the leader of a small group of friends who meet regularly for Bible study, to lead a study in our home. The study I was asked to prepare for included aspects of *'Wisdom'* which can be found in Proverbs. While preparing for the study, it occurred to me (for the first time) that the seven pillars of Wisdom (they are described in Proverbs 9:1–6) have a vivid similarity to the Bible's first account of

Creation and the seven festivals of the Lord (the Jewish people's seven annual festivals). Having seen these three connections, I felt it appropriate if I were to include them in my final lecture for the students in Moldova.

From the feed-back I received from the students – and the members of a church in the Russian part of Moldova where I was invited to speak on my last Sunday in Moldova – I was struck and greatly encouraged by their responses.

After I returned home, I contacted the Editor of Apostolos Publishing – who had earlier published for me two titles – to ask if he would be willing to publish for me this study. The reason I felt to do so is because I know there are many who search the scriptures daily in order for them to learn more about their Saviour, the Lord Jesus – but where should believers in Jesus begin, in the Old Testament, or the New? And for many, I suspect, to begin in the first chapter of Genesis is not the most obvious place to begin? But why, if the Bible is God's book and Jesus is the Alpha and Omega (the beginning and the end) of these two testaments?

In essence I now see these pillars as being an important part of my faith, for they connect Scripture to Scripture in a way I had not previously understood. From my own perception – and I've been a Christian for more than fifty years – these pillars explain what the Bible says about Jesus and what it was that He came to do. His first coming took place about two thousand years ago, but He said He would come again. Perhaps, surprisingly, these seven pillars of Wisdom appear to include important truths we need to understand about His next visit; especially before it happens, so that we may be prepared and ready for His second coming.

David Hamshire

THE BIBLE'S SEVEN PILLARS OF WISDOM

In Proverbs 9:1-6, reference is made to the Bible's *'Seven Pillars of Wisdom'*. These pillars include what is necessary when preparing for a meal – such as a wedding supper.

1. Wisdom has selected a life to be slain.
2. Wisdom has chosen the wine.
3. Wisdom's table has been furnished.
4. Wisdom's servants announce from the highest places of the city: *"Whoever is simple, let him turn in here!"*
5. Wisdom's servants invite others to attend, including, *"Him who lacks understanding."*
6. Wisdom commands: *"Come, eat of my bread and drink of the wine I have mixed."*
7. Wisdom's finale is: *"Forsake foolishness and live, and go in the way of understanding."*

In 2013, I asked the Lord why Passover was the first of the Bible's *'Seven Feasts of the Lord'* – the death of the Passover lambs. It was the order of these seven festivals that I did not understand. A few days later, I asked Janet my wife if she would like a cup of tea. Her reply was, *"Yes please"*, and so I filled the kettle, switched it on, then waited for it to boil.

During the brief silence that ensued, I felt compelled to read Genesis chapter one. Until then, I could not say with any certainty that I understood the Bible's account of Creation, but now as I read, I began to see a portrayal of the seven feasts of the Lord. They are described in Leviticus 23:4-43.

Four years later, in early 2017, when reading in Proverbs about the Bible's seven pillars of Wisdom, I concluded that they are also included in these two events. In fact the three events – seven being the common denominator – appear to be perfect mirror images of each other.

THE FIRST DAY AND PASSOVER

Genesis 1:1–5. *In the beginning, God created the heavens and the earth. The earth was without form and void; and darkness was on the face of the deep. Then God said: "Let there be light"; and there was light. And God saw the light, that it was good; and God divided the light from the darkness. God called the light Day, and the darkness He called Night. So the evening and the morning were the first day.*

The events of the first day may not be as straight–forward as they appear. For example, what is the nature of its light? Clearly it is not the light of the sun, for the sun does not feature until the fourth day. Might this be a way of seeing not only what took place in the beginning, but also what the apostle John once saw: *A new heaven and a new earth ... the holy city, New Jerusalem, coming down out of heaven from God, prepared as a bride adorned for her husband .... The city had no need of the sun or of the moon to shine in it, for the glory of God illuminated it. The Lamb is its light* (Revelation 21:1–2 & 23). The *'Lamb'* which is the *'Light'*, is Jesus.

In 1 John 1:5 we read, *God is light and in Him is no darkness at all.* What is described as having taken place on the first day, is an indication of one of God's many virtues. When light made its first appearance, it displaced the darkness.

Before the children of Israel were set free from slavery in Egypt, God told Moses to tell the people that on the tenth day of their first month, they were to select one-year-old male lambs without blemish (or fault). Four days later, the day of preparation for the Passover (its Hebrew name is *'Pesach'*), the lambs were killed and their blood was struck on the doorposts and lintel of each house as a sign their homes were occupied by God's people. Later, at midnight – a time of darkness – when God passed-over Egypt (Exodus

12:29), for those in the houses marked by the blood of the Passover lambs, they were spared God's judgement.

When Jesus entered Jerusalem on the tenth day of the first month, the same day (John 12:1 & 12), it was because four days later on the eve of Passover, Jesus was to become the *'Lamb of God'* who would take away the sin of those who trust in Him. The night before Jesus died, He prayed, *"And now O Father, glorify Me together with Yourself, with the glory which I had with You before the world was ... for You loved Me before the foundation of the world"* (John 17:5 & 24). Jesus, the *'Alpha and the Omega'* (Revelation 22:13), knew that His earth-bound mission was coming to an end.

Remembering how Jesus is portrayed in day one of Creation – *"Let there be light"* – the evening before the *'Light of the World'* was to be extinguished at Passover, Jesus explained what was about to happen to Him. *"A little while longer the light is with you. Walk while you have the light, lest darkness overtake you; he who walks in darkness does not know where he is going. While you have the light, believe in the light, that you may become sons of light"* (John 12:35-36). Earlier Jesus had said: *"I am the light of the world. He who follows me shall not walk in darkness but shall have the light of life"* (John 8:12). Jesus, therefore, *'The Light of the World'*, is linked to the first day and Passover (when God's people were set-free from their darkest hour), the time when Jesus died.

The appearance of light on the first day, explains the context of how Jesus became, *'The Lamb slain from the foundation of the world'* (Revelation 13:8). It was that He might take upon Himself the darkness of our sin, and so the death of Jesus at Passover corresponds to the first pillar of Wisdom – **'She has slaughtered her meat'**. I realise this is a harsh saying, but it is also confirmed in Isaiah. *He was led as a lamb to the slaughter* (Isaiah 53:7). In order to save us, Jesus had to die.

THE SECOND DAY AND
THE FEAST OF UNLEAVENED BREAD

Genesis 1:6–8. *Then God said, "Let there be a firmament in the midst of the waters, and let it divide the waters from the waters." Thus God made the firmament, and divided the waters which were under the firmament from the waters which were above the firmament; and it was so. And God called the firmament heaven. So the evening and the morning were the second day.*

Biblically, where the number two occurs, it often indicates separation, or division, for it is the first number which can be divided. On the second day, God divided the waters by means of a firmament, which He then called *'Heaven'*. Later, Jesus taught His disciples there is a separation/division between those who believe in God, and those who do not believe. Because of this, there will always be consequences.

Our freedom to choose – *"Life and good,* [or] *death and evil"* (Deuteronomy 30:15) – is related to what God did on the second day, and division is what Jewish people do when they observe the festival of Unleavened Bread, when they remove all traces of leaven (yeast) from their homes – for leaven is symbolic of sin. In the same way to what happens when you add yeast to bread flour; sin can permeate a person's life, both physically and spiritually. Its access is via our desires, our sight and our pride (1 John 2:16).

God's instructions for the keeping of the feast of Unleavened Bread were given before the children of Israel left Egypt. In Exodus 12:16–17, we read: *"On the first day there shall be a holy convocation, and on the seventh day there shall be a holy convocation for you. No manner of work shall be done on them; but that which everyone must eat – that only may be prepared by you. So you shall observe the Feast of Unleavened Bread, for on this same day I will have brought your armies out of the land of Egypt. Therefore you shall observe this day throughout your generations as an everlasting ordinance."* Note this is an everlasting command.

The unleavened bread used today to recall this ordinance is called *'Matzah'*, and what is noteworthy is it is perforated, with its perforations lining up in rows. The use of *'Matzah'* reminds us of how the hands and feet of Jesus were pierced by nails. After Jesus had died, His side was pierced with a spear and blood and water flowed from Him (John 19:34). In Psalm 22:16, we read, *They pierced My hands and My feet.* And in Isaiah 53:5, *But He was wounded for our transgressions, He was bruised for our iniquities; the chastisement for our peace was upon Him, and by His stripes we are healed.* Finally, in Revelation 1:7, when referring to His return, we read: *Behold, He is coming with the clouds, and every eye will see Him, even they who pierced Him. And all the tribes of the earth will mourn because of Him.*

The second feast, Unleavened Bread, is linked to the division God created on the second day, when He divided the waters. Later, God repeated this same act of division when He divided the Red Sea to enable the children of Israel to leave Egypt following their four hundred years of slavery (Genesis 15:13 & Acts 7:6). These examples of the division of water are also pictures of water baptism. When a person who believes in Jesus is baptised, the water will be divided.

In His sermon on the mount, Jesus spoke of two gates. (As we have seen, two can equal division). *"Enter by the narrow gate; for wide is the gate and broad the way that leads to destruction, and there are many who go in by it. Because narrow is the gate and difficult is the way which leads to life, and there are few who find it"* (Matthew 7:13–14).

The second day and the second festival points to how Jesus who was righteous, died for the unrighteous, that He might bring us into a relationship with Himself and His Father.

Paul the apostle also knew about this need for division. *Do you not know that a little leaven leavens the whole lump? Therefore, purge out the old leaven, that you may be a new lump, since you truly are unleavened. For indeed Christ, our Passover, was sacrificed for us. Therefore let us keep the feast, not with the old leaven, nor with the leaven of malice and wickedness, but with the unleavened bread of sincerity and truth* (1 Corinthians 5:6–8).

By using the metaphors of leavened and unleavened bread, Paul explained how that when Jesus died, His death enabled us to be cleansed from our sin and to lead a life of righteousness. Because Jesus was without sin, He is the fulfilment of the festival of Unleavened Bread. Jesus said of Himself: *"I am the bread of life"* (John 6:35).

Before Jesus died and to confirm He was without sin, Pilate (at the time the leading authority in Jerusalem and having questioned/examined Jesus as the high priest would have examined the Passover lamb for any defects before sanctioning its death) said of Him no less than three times: *"I find no fault in Him"* (John 18:38 & 19:4 & 6).

At a wedding in Cana of Galilee, Jesus gave instructions for the servants to fill six large pots with water (John 2:1–11). (Six in the Hebrew idiom is the number for mankind and reminds us of the six days when God created the heavens and the earth). After the vessels had been filled, Jesus then turned the water into wine. When the wine was poured out, it was said that the new wine tasted much better than the old. This miracle – which involved water being changed into wine – explains how Jesus can change a person's life.

When we invite Jesus into our lives, our new way of life has been designed to be much better than the old, because Jesus – like the wine at the wedding – poured out His life-blood.

Red wine, which in biblical terms represents the life-blood of Jesus – *"For the life of the flesh is in the blood, and I have given it to you upon the alter to make atonement for your souls; for it is the blood that makes atonement for the soul"* (Leviticus 17:11) – is what believers in Jesus drink at the meal of Holy Communion, when they remember Him and His dying for them on a cross in Jerusalem.

The usage of red wine is not unlike how when the children of Israel emerged from their four hundred years of slavery in Egypt, that Moses was seen as their saviour as he went before them when they crossed the divided *'Red Sea'*.

The second pillar of Wisdom, as it states in Proverbs 9:2, is, **'She has mixed her wine'.** This mixing of wine equates to the blood of Jesus which, according to the apostle John, can cleanse (divide) us from our sin (1 John 1:7).

For those who may not be familiar with this mixing of wine (by a factor of two) and its importance, this will become much clearer when we come to and consider:

1. The sixth day of Creation.

2. The sixth appointed time of remembrance (the Lord's Day of Atonement).

3. The sixth pillar of Wisdom.

However, before we get to the sixth day, there are still three days for us to consider – the third, fourth and fifth days.

THE THIRD DAY AND THE FEAST OF FIRSTFRUITS

Genesis 1:9–13. Then God said, "Let the waters under the heavens be gathered together into one place, and let the dry land appear"; and it was so. And God called the dry land Earth, and the gathering together of the waters He called Seas. And God saw that it was good. Then God said. "Let the earth bring forth grass, the herb that yields seed, and the fruit tree that yields fruit according to its kind, whose seed is in itself, on the earth"; and it was so. And God saw that it was good. So the evening and the morning were the third day.

For botanists, this statement about plants producing seed and fruit on the third day, before the sun and moon make their appearance a day later (on the fourth day) to control the Earth's seasons, may seem impossible. But this is not so, not if the third day points to the resurrection of Jesus after He had spent three days and three nights in the tomb.

The number three is widely recognized in Scripture as being the number representing resurrection, and confirms why Jesus had to remain in the tomb for three days and three nights before rising from the dead.

Many saw Jesus' resurrection as being impossible, however, Jesus said to Martha, *"I am the resurrection and the life, He who believes in Me, though he may die, he shall live"* (John 11:25). Later, Jesus said to His disciples, *"I am the vine, you are the branches. He who abides in Me, and I in him, bears much fruit; for without Me you can do nothing"* (John 15:5). When Jesus spoke of His resurrection and His disciples as bearing fruit (other people); each recalled the third day.

The resurrection of Jesus is most likely to have taken place at the time of the third Hebrew festival, Firstfruits, for it was on the third day that *'first-fruits'* was observed for the first time. The apostle Paul suggests this. *But now is Christ risen from the dead and has become the firstfruits of those who have fallen asleep* (1 Corinthians 15:20).

Jesus also indicated this. *"As Jonah was three days and three nights in the belly of the great fish; so will the Son of Man be three days and three nights in the heart of the earth"* (Matthew 12:40). It was on the third day of Creation that God gathered the seas, then the dry land. It was the same period of days, the same elements and the same sequence that Jonah was in the sea and Jesus was in the tomb.

In his book *'Gleanings in Genesis'*, Arthur Walkington Pink writes: *"In the third day's work our Lord's resurrection is typically set forth. Beyond doubt, that which is foreshadowed on the third day's work is resurrection. It was on the third day that our Lord rose again from the dead 'according to the Scriptures'. Do we not have in Genesis one, the first of these Scriptures, the primitive picture of our Lord's resurrection?"*

Luke wrote it was after He died and on the third day when Jesus was at a table with two of His disciples, that He made Himself known to them (Luke 24:30–31). The disciples then said to each other: *"Did not our heart burn within us while He talked with us on the road, and while He opened the Scriptures to us?"* (Luke 24:32). This incident recalls Psalm 23:5. *You prepare a table before me in the presence of my enemies.* At the time of His rising from death, Jesus' enemies believed they could prevent His resurrection by sealing His tomb and guarding it. Thankfully, they were mistaken.

The third pillar of Wisdom, **'She has also furnished her table'**, is confirmed first by the victorious meal Jesus shared in at a *'table'* when He rose from the dead on the third day. But also, a table is being *'furnished'* for His wedding supper, when His people will sit with Him as His bride.

THE FOURTH DAY AND THE FEAST OF WEEKS

Genesis 1:14–19. *Then God said, "Let there be lights in the firmament of the heavens to divide the day from the night; and let them be for signs and seasons, and for days and years; and let them be for lights in the firmament of the heavens to give light on the earth"; and it was so.*

Then God made two great lights; the greater light to rule the day, and the lesser light to rule the night. He made the stars also. And God saw that it was good. So the evening and the morning were the fourth day.

It is from the sun which gives light and heat during the day, the moon which gives light and beauty at night, and the tilt of the earth from its vertical axis, that God has given to us the four seasons. And it is from the four seasons that we derive the harvests and from these we obtain our food. If this was not the case, much of the created order would die.

Jesus said, *"The kingdom of God is as if a man should scatter seed on the ground, and should sleep by night and rise by day, and the seed should sprout and grow, he himself does not know how. For the earth yields crops by itself: first the blade, then the head, after that the full grain in the head. But when the grain ripens, immediately he puts in the sickle, because the harvest has come"* (Mark 4:26–29).

Jesus said the kingdom of God is like a harvest field, and the earth's harvest is only made possible by the appearance of the sun and the moon which took place on the fourth day. The fourth Jewish festival – Feast of Weeks – is when Jewish people give thanks for their wheat harvest. It was also at this time that Jesus sent the Holy Spirit to His disciples, that they might become workers in the world (together with His Father) which He had created (Hebrews 1:2). Jesus said to them: *"The harvest is truly plentiful, but the laborers are few. Therefore pray the Lord of the harvest to send out laborers into His harvest"* (Matthew 9:37-38).

The fourth Jewish festival, the Feast of Weeks, is celebrated seven weeks and one day (fifty days) after the Jewish people have celebrated their feast of Firstfruits. In Hebrew this festival is called *'Shavuot'*. In Greek it is called *'Pentecost'*.

When the disciples were filled with the Holy Spirit on the day of Pentecost, about one hundred and twenty of them were in gathered in Jerusalem (Acts 1:15). When Solomon dedicated the first temple in Jerusalem, one hundred and twenty priests sounded their trumpets and gave thanks to God and said: *"For He is good, for His mercy endures forever"* (2 Chronicles 5:12-13). It was then that *'The glory of the LORD filled the house of God'*. This *'Glory of the LORD'* which descended in the days of Solomon on the house of God on the first day of the Jewish Feast of Tabernacles, was not unlike that which took place at the time of Pentecost, and in the same city, Jerusalem.

When Peter spoke on the day of Pentecost, he quoted from the book of the prophet Joel about what he and the other disciples had just experienced. *"But this is what was spoken by the prophet Joel: 'And it shall come to pass in the last days, says God, that I will pour out my Spirit on all flesh...'"* (Acts 2:16-17). Continuing, Peter said: *"I will show wonders in heaven above and signs in the earth beneath: Blood and fire and vapor of smoke. The sun shall be turned into darkness and the moon into blood, before the coming of the great and awesome day of the LORD. And it shall come to pass that whoever calls on the name of the LORD shall be saved'"* (Acts 2:19-21). Although Joel's prophecy (quoted by Peter on the day of Pentecost) refers to the sun being darkened and the moon being turned into blood (red), earlier in this same prophecy it refers to: *"The threshing floors will be full of wheat and the vats shall overflow with new wine and oil"* (Joel 2:24). Joel's prophecy links Israel's wheat harvest to the sun and the moon, which according to Genesis 1:14 can at certain times act as *'Signs'* for God's people.

To His disciples, Jesus said: *"Go into all the world and preach the gospel to every creature. He who believes and is baptized will be saved; but he who does not believe will be condemned"* (Mark 16:15-16). The disciples, however, were told to wait until they had received the Holy Spirit. Jesus said to them: *"Behold, I send the Promise of My Father upon you; but tarry in the city of Jerusalem until you are endued with power from on high"* (Luke 24:49). Having waited, Peter then explained to the first invited guests, the Jewish people, the Gospel.

The fourth pillar of Wisdom states: **'She has sent out her maidens, she cries out from the highest places of the city, "Whoever is simple, let him turn in here!"'** Is this *'City'* Jerusalem? It certainly appears so, for Wisdom's instruction (the Holy Spirit) links Jerusalem as the city where:

1. God has chosen to place His name. *"Yet I have chosen Jerusalem that My name may be there..."* (2 Chronicles 6:6).

2. The disciples (who were Jewish) were filled with the Holy Spirit on the day of Pentecost (Feast of Weeks).

3. After Peter had preached the Gospel first to the Jews, approximately 3,000 of them came to faith in Jesus and acknowledged Him as their Messiah (Acts 2:40).

NB. In Semitic languages, such as the Hebrew language, the gender for *'Wisdom'* and *'Spirit'* – the Holy Spirit – and those who will attend the *'Marriage Supper of the Lamb'*, is female.

THE FIFTH DAY AND THE FEAST OF TRUMPETS

Genesis 1:20-23. On the fifth day – *Then God said: "Let the waters abound with an abundance of living creatures, and let birds fly above the earth across the face of the firmament of the heavens." So God created great sea creatures and every living thing that moves, with which the waters abounded, according to their kind, and every winged bird according to its kind. And God saw that it was good. And God blessed them, saying: "Be fruitful and multiply, and fill the waters in the seas, and let birds multiply on the earth." So the evening and the morning were the fifth day.'*

The fifth Jewish festival, the Feast of Trumpets, is observed in the Bible calendar on the first day of the seventh month. This day includes, *"...at the beginning of your months, you shall blow the trumpets over your burnt offerings and over the sacrifices of your peace offerings; and they shall be a memorial for you before your God: I am the LORD your God"* (Numbers 10:10). In Hebrew understanding, five is the number for grace, God's goodness and His mercy.

Jewish tradition teaches us that at the time of the Feast of Trumpets, was when Abraham took Isaac to Mount Moriah and there Abraham took the wood which Isaac had carried on his back and prepared an altar to offer up his son to God. As Abraham was about to slay his son, the angel of the LORD intervened and told Abraham not to kill Isaac. It was then that, *Abraham lifted his eyes and looked, and there behind him was a ram caught in a thicket by its horns. So Abraham went and took the ram and offered it up for a burnt offering instead of his son* (Genesis 22:13).

This Jewish/Hebrew tradition is a constant reminder of how Jesus carried His cross made of wood on his back, and a cruel crown of thorns was placed on His head.

At the Feast of Trumpets, the sound of the trumpet is also a reminder that if we obey God (as Abraham obeyed God), we will be saved from death. In today's terms (like Isaac), it means being saved from the consequences of sin, i.e., death.

God's command on the fifth day to the sea creatures and the birds to fill the seas and earth by multiplying, was mirrored precisely in the final command Jesus gave to His disciples. *"Go therefore and make disciples of all the nations* [multiply]*, baptizing them in the name of the Father and of the Son and of the Holy Spirit"* (Matthew 28:19).

At the time when the disciples were filled with the Holy Spirit (Feast of Weeks), they were gathered in the heights of Jerusalem, and from there they went out and preached the Gospel to Jews only. A few weeks later, Peter went up to the roof of a house in Joppa to rest (Joppa means *'Beauty'*), and it was there that God spoke to him and said it was now time for him (a Jew) to go to the Gentiles. Peter, in responding to God's calling, then went to the house of a Gentile, Cornelius, a centurion of the Italian Regiment, and preached the Gospel to those gathered (Acts 10:1). To Peter's utter amazement, as Cornelius believed, the Holy Spirit descended upon him.

Peter's experience mirrored the fifth day and the fifth feast, the Feast of Trumpets, for the disciples to be as Jesus had instructed them: *"...you shall be witnesses to Me in Jerusalem, and in all Judea and Samaria, and to the end of the earth"* (Acts 1:8). The reason for this command is in Revelation 14:6–7. *Then I saw another angel flying in the midst of heaven, having the everlasting gospel to preach to those who dwell on the earth – to every nation, tribe, tongue, and people – saying with a loud voice* (like the sound of the trumpet), *"Fear God and give glory to Him, for the hour of His judgment has come; and worship Him who made heaven and earth, the sea and the springs of water."* NB. The earth and sea/water.

The fifth pillar of Wisdom – **'As for him who lacks understanding, she says to him...'** – indicates that a new list of guests is to be invited. This equates to the Gentiles who by nature had not known God – the first case was Cornelius and those of his household who welcomed Peter into the home of Cornelius to explain the Gospel – that they are now invited to join the first invited guests (the Jewish people who believe in Jesus) at His marriage supper.

Like Peter, the apostle Paul also came to realise it was God's intention for Gentiles to be invited, to become with the Jews; the *'Bride of Christ'*. Paul wrote: *Therefore remember that you, once Gentiles in the flesh ... that at that time you were without Christ, being aliens from the commonwealth of Israel and strangers from the covenants of promise, having no hope and without God in the world.*

But now in Christ Jesus you who once were far off have been brought near by the blood of Christ. For He Himself is our peace, who has made both one, and has broken down the middle wall of separation, having abolished in His flesh the enmity ... so as to create in Himself one new man from the two, thus making peace, and that He might reconcile them both to God in one body through the cross, thereby putting to death the enmity (Ephesians 2:11–16).

When the apostle John was given detailed information about the *'Marriage Supper of the Lamb'* – and possibly unknown to John at the time his recording of these future events were to be included in the final pages of the New Testament – John wrote: *'He said to me "Write: 'Blessed are those who are called to the marriage supper of the Lamb!'"* (Those who are the *'called'*, include Jews and the Gentiles). *And He said to me, "These are the true sayings of God"'* (Revelation 19:9). John was then told to: *"Worship God. For the testimony of Jesus is the spirit of prophecy"* (Revelation 19:10).

THE SIXTH DAY AND THE DAY OF ATONEMENT

Genesis 1:24 & 26–27. Then God said, "Let the earth bring forth the living creature according to its kind; cattle and creeping thing and beast of the earth, each according to its kind;" and it was so. Then God said, "Let Us make man in Our image, according to Our likeness; let them have dominion over the fish of the sea, over the birds of the air, and over the cattle, over all the earth and over every creeping thing that creeps on the earth." So God created man in His own image; in the image of God He created Him; male and female He created them.

Then God saw everything that He had made, and indeed it was very good. So the evening and the morning were the sixth day (Genesis 1:31).

The fact the Bible states *'man'* was made on the sixth day, and the Day of Atonement is the sixth appointed time (in Hebrew, *'Yom Kippur'*), suggests an additional importance is associated with these two events – the birth of Jesus. The reason is because Jesus was destined to become our High Priest, and to fulfil what Aaron was appointed to do in the Tabernacle's Holy-of-Holies. This is why the sixth day and the sixth observance, the Day of Atonement, are inseparable.

When God spoke to Moses and told him how Aaron his brother was to approach God in the Holy-of-Holies, God said to him: *"Tell Aaron your brother not to come at just any time into the Holy Place inside the veil, before the mercy seat which is on the ark, lest he die; for I will appear in the cloud above the mercy seat"* (Leviticus 16:2).

Clearly from these instructions, it was essential for Aaron to obey God. Not to have done so, and Aaron would have died. Why was it important for Aaron to observe the procedure laid down by God for the keeping of the Day of Atonement? It was because this *'Day"* was always going to be a part of God's plan for His Son, and so the foretelling of His birth – the time when He entered this world in His meekness – is to be found in the Scriptures that Jesus so often referred to; in the writings of Moses, the prophets and the Psalms.

In Margaret Barker's book, *'Christmas, the original story'*, Barker refers to Philo who saw the two accounts of Creation as being different. Philo describes how he understood Genesis. *"Genesis 1:26 describes the heavenly Adam, made in the image and after the likeness of God. Genesis 2:7 describes the man formed from dust. There are two types of men; the one a heavenly man* [Jesus], *the other an earthly* [Adam]" (Philo, *'Allegorical Interpretation'*). Barker uses theological logic to reason that the only day in the Hebrew Scriptures for which it would have been suitable for Jesus to have been born, was on the *'Lord's Day of Atonement'*.

The apostle John describes how when he was in exile on the island of Patmos, he heard a voice. John then describes what he heard. *"I was in the Spirit on the Lord's Day, and I heard behind me a loud voice, as of a trumpet"* (Revelation 1:10). The voice John heard was the voice of Jesus.

I have heard it said John indicates that this was the first day of the week, referred to by some as the being the *'The Lord's Day'*. Is this likely? In the language of the Complete Jewish Bible, the Hebrew rendering of this statement is reversed. Its description is: *'The Day of the Lord'*. The way John refers to this day as *'The Day of the Lord'*, and how Jesus appeared in His Majesty (*'King of Kings'*) and spoke with a loud voice, I suspect it may well have been the Day of Atonement, for John would have known the importance of keeping this *'Day'* special. Being *'in the Spirit on the Day of the Lord'* – the Day of Atonement – would have been quite natural for John.

In Paul's letter to believers in Philippi, Paul refers to Jesus as God's Son, but also as being born as a man. *"Christ Jesus ... who being in the form of God, did not consider it robbery to be equal with God, but made Himself of no reputation, taking the form of a bondservant, and coming in the likeness of men* [at His birth]. *And being found in appearance as a man, He humbled Himself and became obedient to the point of death, even the death of the cross"* (Philippians 2:5-8). Does this mean that when Jesus was born in Bethlehem, He became less than God? No, of course not, *"For in Him dwells all the fullness of the Godhead bodily"* (Colossians 2:9).

To observe these links (the sixth day of Creation, the Day of Atonement and the birth of Jesus) is to see that there is also a fourth link. The sixth pillar of Wisdom so clearly points to Jesus, for its instruction is something which Christians have observed for nearly two thousand years: **"Come, eat of my bread, and drink of the wine I have mixed."**

This mixing of wine goes back to when God told Moses how the children of Israel were to observe the Day of Atonement. First, the death of a young bull was presented as an offering for Aaron and his family. Aaron then sprinkled some of its blood on the Mercy Seat of the Ark of the Covenant. Next, a goat was slain as a sin offering for the people and some of its blood was also sprinkled on the Mercy Seat, to mix with the blood of the young bull. This mixing of blood – *repeated seven times* (Leviticus 16:11-16) – was done to show how the bull's blood which Aaron offered as a token for himself as high priest, was to mix with the goat's blood which died for the sins of God's people. Much later, this pattern of two bloods mixing as one – Jesus who was the *'Son of God'* and also *'Son of Man'* – was repeated when Jesus died on the cross. Therefore, and not surprisingly, when Jesus died, a centurion who was an official witness to His death said of Jesus: *"Truly this Man was the Son of God!"* (Mark 15:39).

The Incarnation – God becoming Man – is the first of the two most important events in history, for it was when Jesus entered this world through the veil dividing heaven and earth. At the end of His life, the second most important event took place, for it was when Jesus died that the veil of the Temple was torn in two. These two events show that we now have access to the throne-room of God (Hebrews 4:16).

The apostle John referred to God in human flesh when he wrote: *In the beginning was the Word* [Jesus] *and the Word was with God, and the Word was God. He was in the beginning with God* (John 1:1-2). Concerning this statement, Tom Wright in his commentary on John's gospel writes: *John probably expects some readers to see that this opening passage says about Jesus, what some writers had said about 'Wisdom'. Many Jewish teachers had grappled with the age-old questions: 'How can the one true God be both different from the world and active within the world? How can He be remote, holy and detached, and also intimately present?'*

The answer to these questions is to be found in *'Wisdom'*, for as Jesus said to His disciples about where He had come from and to where He was going: *"I came forth from the Father and have come into the world. Again, I leave the world and go to the Father"* (John 16:28). In other words, Jesus was both God and man in the one body. Jesus also said to His disciple Philip: *"He who has seen me has seen the Father"* (John 14:9).

The sixth pillar of Wisdom also anticipated the last meal Jesus was to share with His disciples, in what He said about the bread and the wine. The bread, *"This is My body which is given for you."* The wine, *"This cup is the new covenant in My blood which is shed for you"* (Luke 22:19-20). Once again, the words of Jesus and the biblical typology remind us of the prophetic words found in Proverbs 9:5. **"Come, eat of my bread, and drink of the wine I have mixed."**

The act of taking Holy Communion, however, is only part of the story, it is its introduction. What comes next will be the wedding supper, because Jesus, God's Son, gave up His earthly/bodily life that we may have eternal life.

As a prelude to this last of all wedding suppers – and I believe it is wrong to speculate about its timing or the way in which it will take place – for Jews and Gentiles who respond to *'Wisdom's Invitation'*, they will eventually experience what was later revealed to the apostle John.

Then one of the elders answered saying to me [John], *"Who are these arrayed in white robes* [wedding garments]*, and where did they come from?" And I said to him, "Sir, you know." So he said to me, "These are the ones who come out of the great tribulation, and washed their robes and made them white in the blood of the Lamb.*

Therefore they are before the throne of God, and serve Him day and night in His temple [God's *'Tabernacle'*]*. And He who sits on the throne will dwell among them. They shall neither hunger any more* [food] *nor thirst anymore*[drink]*; the sun shall not strike them, nor any heat; for the Lamb who is in the midst of the throne* [Jesus] *will shepherd them and lead them to living waters. And God will wipe away every tear from their eyes"* (Revelation 7:13–17).

This mention of *'living waters'* is one we will encounter again, during the seventh day. Meanwhile: *Therefore we also, since we are surrounded by so great a cloud of witnesses, let us lay aside every weight, and the sin which so easily ensnares us, and let us run with endurance the race that is set before us, looking unto Jesus, the author and finisher of our faith, who for the joy that was set before Him endured the cross, despising the shame, and has sat down at the right hand of the throne of God* (Hebrews12:1–2).

THE SEVENTH DAY AND THE FEAST OF TABERNACLES

Genesis 2:1-3. *Thus the heavens and the earth, and all the host of them, were finished. And on the seventh day God ended His work which He had done, and He rested on the seventh day from all His work which He had done. Then God blessed the seventh day and sanctified it* [God made it holy], *because in it He rested from all His work which God had created and made.*

Day seven parallels the seventh Jewish festival, the Feast of Tabernacles (in Hebrew, *'Succot'*), for it is, *"The Feast of Ingathering at the end of the year, when you have gathered in the fruit of your labors from the field"* (Exodus 23:16). After gathering in their final harvest, the fruits, nuts and berries, for Jewish people, it is a time for the giving thanks and for rest – as God blessed the seventh day and He rested.

This festival is also known as the Feast of Booths, the time when Jewish people build temporary shelters to dwell in during the seven days of this festival. These booths are a reminder of the temporary shelters they lived in during the forty years they were wandering in the wilderness, before they entered the Promised Land in the days of Joshua.

The Promised Land was where Abraham once lived, and where he and his family also lived in tents. *By faith Abraham obeyed when he was called to go out to the place which he would receive as an inheritance. And he went out not knowing where he was going. By faith he dwelt in the land of promise as in a foreign country, dwelling in tents with Isaac and Jacob, the heirs with him of the same promise; for he waited for the city which has foundations, whose builder and maker is God* (Hebrews 11:8-10).

The city Abraham was waiting for was the city of the living God, the heavenly Jerusalem. In this city, it is expected that Abraham will join with *...an innumerable company of angels, to the general assembly and church* [community] *of the firstborn who are registered in heaven, to God the Judge of all, to the spirits of just men made perfect, to Jesus the Mediator of the new covenant, and to the blood of sprinkling that speaks better things than that of Abel* (Hebrews 12:22-24).

For Abraham and all of God's people, for those who have trusted in God and in His Son the Lord Jesus and have said "Yes" to Wisdom's invitation, when they have finished the work they have been given to do, their rest is assured. In Hebrews this rest is described as entering His rest; but also, *"Be diligent to enter that rest"* (Hebrews 4:10 & 11).

In Matthew's gospel (11:25), Matthew recorded a prayer of Jesus. *"I thank you, Father, Lord of heaven and earth, that you have hidden these things from the wise and prudent and have revealed them to babes."* His prayer, addressing His Father as *'Lord of heaven and earth'*, is reminiscent of Moses using these same words when he spoke to the children of Israel about choosing life or death (Deuteronomy 30:19). Prior to this prayer, Jesus rebuked those who would not repent; but then He invited those who did repent, *"Come to Me, all you who labor and are heavy laden, and I will give you rest. Take My yoke upon you and learn from Me, for I am gentle and lowly in heart, and you will find rest for your souls. For my yoke is easy and My burden is light"* (Matthew 11:28-30). Jesus is conscious of the needs of those who follow Him – especially those who suffer for Him – to enter their rest.

Recalling what is anticipated to *'rest'* with Jesus, Jesus also said to His disciples: *"Let not your heart be troubled; you believe in God, believe also in Me. In my Father's house are many mansions; if it were not so, I would have told you. I go to prepare a place for you. And if I go and prepare a place for you, I will come again and receive you to Myself; that where I am, there you may be also"* (John 14:1-3).

The temporary shelters Jewish people construct and use during their *'sabbath-rest'* (Leviticus 23:39) at the time of the Feast of Tabernacles, when they give thanks for their final harvest, corresponds to the many mansions that Jesus spoke of during His final hours with His disciples. Earlier, when Jesus went up to Jerusalem to attend the Feast of Tabernacles, it was, *On the last day, that great day of the feast, Jesus stood and cried out, saying, "If anyone thirsts, let him come to Me and drink. He who believes in Me, as the Scripture has said, out of his heart will flow rivers of living water"* (John 7:37-38).

The seventh pillar of Wisdom, **"Forsake foolishness and live, and go in the way of understanding"**, is intended for the simple and those who lack understanding (the fourth and fifth pillars of Wisdom) when they choose *'life'* and follow Jesus, rather than choosing foolishness and death.

To the believers in Corinth, Paul wrote mainly to those who lacked understanding (Gentile believers). *For you see your calling, brethren, that not many wise according to the flesh, not many mighty, not many noble are called. But God has chosen the foolish things of the world to put to shame the wise, and God has chosen the weak things of the world to put to shame the things which are mighty; and the base things of the world and the things which are despised God has chosen, and the things which are not, to bring to nothing the things which are, that no flesh should glory in His presence. But of Him you are in Christ Jesus, who became for us wisdom from God – and righteousness and sanctification and redemption – that as it is written, "He who glories, let him glory in the LORD"* (I Corinthians 1:26 – 31).

The invitation of the Holy Spirit (*'Wisdom'*) is for both Jews and Gentiles to attend the *'Marriage Supper of the Lamb of God'*, so that when the Bridegroom appears, the Lord Jesus, they will be able to have fellowship with Him at His table.

Included as part of John's vision as described in the book of Revelation, there is a description of what it will be like for those who have made themselves ready for the Bridegroom. *Here is the patience of the saints; here are those who keep the commandments of God and the faith of Jesus. Then I heard a voice from heaven saying to me, "Write: 'Blessed are the dead who die in the Lord from now on.'" "Yes," says the Spirit* [Wisdom], *"That they may rest from their labors, and their works follow them"* (Revelation 14:12-13).

When God finished His work on the sixth day, then He rested on the seventh day for His work was complete (as Jewish people rest at the time of the Feast of Tabernacles after their final harvest has been gathered in), so, too, for those who have entrusted their lives to Jesus and have sought to do God's will, they can look forward to the time which can only be described as a well-earned rest.

The illustration Jesus used when He spoke to the Pharisees and priests about His kingdom was of a wedding supper. Jesus said to them: *"The kingdom of heaven is like a certain king who arranged a marriage for his son, and sent out his servants to call those who were invited to the wedding; and they were not willing to come."*

"Again, he sent out other servants, saying, 'Tell those who are invited, "See, I have prepared my dinner; my oxen and fatted cattle are killed, and all things are ready. Come to the wedding."' But they made light of it and went their ways, one to his own farm, another to his business. And the rest seized his servants, treated them spitefully, and killed them."

"But when the king heard about it, he was furious. And he sent out his armies, destroyed those murderers, and burned their city. Then he said to his servants, 'The wedding is ready, but those who were invited were not worthy. Therefore go into the highways, and as many as you find, invite to the wedding. So those servants went out into the highways and gathered together all whom they found, both bad and good."

"And the wedding hall was filled with guests. But when the king came in to see the guests, he saw a man there who did not have on a wedding garment. So he said to him, 'Friend, how did you come in here without a wedding garment?' And he was speechless. Then the king said to his servants, 'Bind him hand and foot, take him away, and cast him into outer darkness; there will be weeping and gnashing of teeth.' For many are called, but few are chosen" (Matthew 22:1-14)

In this description of His *'Marriage Supper'*, Jesus used this parable to explain what will eventually take place, and how if they the Jewish people, the first invited guests, rejected Him, what would happen to them. However, God's plan for Wisdom's invitation was for it to be extended to the rest of the nations, so that if Gentiles believe in Jesus, they will be given the opportunity to attend His Son's Marriage Supper.

Today, Jewish people hold to a tradition that when their Messiah comes, there will be a great feast, such as a wedding feast, and at the end when the wine is drunk, there will be a toast at which it will be said: *"l'chaim!"* [*"To Life!"*].

Sadly, many Jewish people believe God has kept these things hidden from them since the dawn of creation. But this is not the case, for as Jesus once said: *"God so loved the world that He gave His only begotten Son, that whoever believes in Him should not perish but have everlasting life* (John 3:16). This call to life, *"l'chaim!"*, is the seventh pillar of Wisdom.

THE MARRIAGE SUPPER OF THE LAMB

What we have observed in this study is the preparation for Jesus' *'Marriage Supper'*. Its introduction can be found in Genesis 1:1–2:3. Its prophetic fulfilment can be found in the final chapters of John's Revelation.

Wisdom's pillars describe what is planned for this marriage supper, which includes: Food and wine; a table prepared for the guests; two sets of invitations (Jews and Gentiles); a meal fit for a King and those who respond to Wisdom's invitation. Finally, the King's speech: **"Forsake foolishness and live, and go in the way of understanding."** Surely, only God could have pioneered such an amazing plan?

When God told Moses how to construct the *'Tabernacle'*, it was to be made according to a pattern which God showed to Moses when he was on the mountain of God (Exodus 25:40). Later, for the apostle John, the pattern was confirmed after John had seen in a vision the New Jerusalem coming down out of heaven from God, prepared as a bride adorned for her husband. John wrote that he heard a loud voice from heaven saying to him: *"Behold, the tabernacle of God is with men, and He will dwell with them, and they shall be His people. God Himself will be with them and be their God. And God will wipe away every tear from their eyes; there shall be no more pain, for the former things have passed away."* Then He who sat on the throne said, *"Behold, I make all things new."*

And He said to me (John), *"Write, for these words are true and faithful."* And He said to me, *"It is done! I am the Alpha and Omega, the Beginning and the End. I will give of the fountain of the water of life freely to him who thirsts. He who overcomes shall inherit all things, and I will be His God and he shall be My son"* (Revelation 21:3–7).

GOD'S PLAN OF SALVATION

God's eternal plan of salvation is one which has seen many lives changed for the good. Its three facets are: The seven days of Creation, the seven feasts of the Lord, and the seven pillars of Wisdom. A summary can be described as follows:

1. Jesus, who at the time of Passover, the *'Light of the World'* was briefly extinguished at Calvary. When the children of Israel marked their houses with the blood of the Passover lamb, its flesh was then consumed as their evening meal. Before Jesus died at Passover, He said to His disciples, *"The bread that I shall give is My flesh, which I shall give for the life of the world"* (John 6:51). The first pillar of Wisdom is the body of Jesus.

2. Jesus the righteous (Unleavened Bread) surrendered His life for the unrighteous. The second pillar of Wisdom – the life of Jesus, *'for the life of the body is in the blood'* – continues to be recalled when we take the Communion Cup, drink wine and give thanks.

3. Jesus rose from the dead on the third day. This, a *'first-fruit'* sign, confirmed Jesus was God's Son. As proof of His resurrection, Jesus revealed Himself to two of His disciples at a table. The third pillar of Wisdom is of a wedding table that is being prepared.

4. Jesus sent the Holy Spirit to His disciples at the time of the Feast of Weeks (Pentecost) to reap a spiritual harvest among Jewish people (Romans 1:16). They are the first invited guests. This also explains why those who believe in Jesus need the Holy Spirit to dwell within them. The fourth pillar of Wisdom coincided with the time when 3,000 Jewish people responded to the Holy Spirit's invitation.

5. Jesus said, *"Salvation is of the Jews"* (John 4:22). His words recall the preaching of the Gospel by His disciples (Jews) to the Gentiles, as in the sound of the trumpet at the Feast of Trumpets. This inclusiveness of the Gentiles is the fifth pillar of Wisdom.

6. Jesus came (Day of Atonement) to bring us salvation, for salvation leads to access into God's presence. In Hebrews we read: *Let us therefore come boldly to the throne of grace that we may obtain mercy and find grace to help in time of need* (Hebrews 4:16). As we have seen, the mixing of wine (blood) can at first be a mystery, but as the apostle Paul wrote: *God was in Christ reconciling the world to Himself* (2 Corinthians 5:19). The sixth pillar, **"Come, eat of my bread and drink of the wine I have mixed"**, confirms that God was indeed in Christ, both as Himself and as a man.

7. With His last breath, Jesus cried out, *"It is finished!"* (John 19:30). His words recall the seventh day after God had *'finished'* His work – then He rested (Genesis 2:1). For those who serve Jesus, a day is coming when they will have finished the work He has given them to do, and they will then enter their rest. This is similar to what Jewish people do during the Feast of Tabernacles; they rest and give thanks. The seventh pillar of Wisdom is, **"Forsake foolishness and live and go in the way of understanding."**

Thus, included in the Bible's seven pillars of Wisdom, we have a description of what it means to understand why God sent to us His Son, the Lord Jesus. For those who respond to Wisdom's invitation, both Jews and Gentiles, a day is coming when they will join Him at His wedding supper. Meanwhile, we are to work, watch and pray that we may be ready for the time when we will either leave this life, or Jesus returns.

DR. ALLEN WISEMAN

Two weeks after I saw Jesus in Genesis one, I met in Israel, a Canadian-born Jew with a doctorate in Jewish philosophy who informed me he had recently written a pamphlet about the link between the seven days of Creation and the seven feasts of the Lord. His name is Dr. Allen Wiseman.

Dr. Wiseman writes: *"Seven holy appointed times or feasts mark the yearly, Biblical calendar. God initiated the series in Exodus 12, to be fully listed in Leviticus 23. These times represent a pattern of Scripture that begins with the seven days or periods of creation week, that are echoed by the regular weekly cycle, and further elaborated in Israel's deliverance from Egyptian slavery."*

"As creation continues until the end of time, so to do the effects of these seven feasts. Both the repetition of the weekly cycle and the seven yearly holidays, remind us of real past events that also point to the prophetic future. As such, these feasts are more than ordinary holidays. While the regular weekly and yearly cycles ingrain in us a down-to-earth rhythm in life, the linear process gives us an overall perspective that spans from the very beginning of creation to the ultimate completion of God's redemptive purposes. Historically, because the Christian world veered away from its Jewish roots in the early centuries, the larger scope and significance of the Lord's seven feasts were often overlooked, or not sufficiently understood."

Never before (or since) have I been introduced to a Jew who has the initial and surname, A. Wiseman! And the fact this happened in Tel Aviv, Israel, just two weeks after I saw the seven days of Creation and the seven feasts of the Lord as being similar, confirmed (for me) that God is both loving and kind in the way He reveals to us His Word (His Son).

BIBLIOGRAPHY

Barker, Margaret. 'Christmas the Original Story'. Society for Promoting Christian Knowledge (SPCK 2008). 36, Causton Street, London, SW1P 4ST.

Pink, A. W. P. 'Gleanings in Genesis'. (Watchmaker, 1951).

Stern, David H. 'Complete Jewish Bible'. (Jewish New Testament Publications, Inc. Clarksville, Maryland USA. Jerusalem Israel).

Wiseman, A. 'The Feasts – Seven, Holy, Appointed Times of The Lord'.

Wright, Nicholas Thomas. 'John for Everyone'. Society for Promoting Christian Knowledge (SPCK). 36, Causton Street, London, SW1P 4ST. Westminster John Knox Press.

HEBREW FOUNDATIONS OF THE CHRISTIAN FAITH

If you have been helped in any way by this study, then my book, 'HEBREW FOUNDATIONS OF THE CHRISTIAN FAITH', may also be of assistance. It is available from Amazon's web-site. The study in this book is an extension of the final study in this earlier book.

Niall MacTaggart's comments are taken from the Foreword for this book.

When I was invited to read the manuscript for this book, I was impressed on a number of levels. David's book gives a foundation upon which the new believer and student of the Bible can gain biblical orientation which points to Jesus Christ. The presence of the Holy Spirit and the kingdom of God are themes which can transform the course of our study, and David's book will, with certainty, be helpful in equipping believers in living fully in God's economy.

The employment in this book of induction questions – to draw in the student to dialogue and thinking about the topics and the ramifications thereof – is important if we are to see God reveal His Word to men and women, and not only pass on something of what we have learnt; though it may be perfectly valid.

I believe the use of this book would be a wonderful complement to any syllabus of teaching and education in a seminary or Bible school setting. David's book gives form without bondage, freedom without license, and sends the right message of a biblical witness to the living Lord Jesus.

Niall MacTaggart
Spruce Grove, Alberta, Canada

ISRAEL RESTORED

My other book which is also available from Amazon's website – *'ISRAEL RESTORED'* – has been written to provide a biblical focus for the restoration of the Jewish people to the Promised Land. It is the land which God promised to give to Abraham and his descendants as an everlasting possession.

Richard Sexton's comments are taken from the Foreword for this book.

The mention of 'Israel' usually provokes a reaction of some sort. In today's world, the reaction is often negative, with many regarding the nation of Israel as an obstacle to peace.

This book has been written by someone who is a man of strong passions – especially when it comes to the Jews and their nation. David Hamshire has a passion which drives him to discover a true and an eternal viewpoint with which to regard Israel. In looking for arguments to establish his belief in the central place that Israel plays in the purposes of God, David examines Scripture with the eye of a detective, and having found gold nuggets of truth, he then seeks to substantiate them by looking at the history of Israel the nation and the Jews as a people.

'ISRAEL RESTORED' is an argument for the place of Israel in the heart of God, which is detailed and persuasive. David presents a coordinated stream of scriptural support for the survival of Israel against all odds and the place of Israel in these end-times. I commend this book to you.

Richard G. Sexton
Bath, England

www.ingramcontent.com/pod-product-compliance
Lightning Source LLC
Chambersburg PA
CBHW061312040426
42444CB00010B/2601